Eastern European Poets Series #40

Kholin 66: Diaries and Poems
Copyright © 2017, 2018 by Liudmila Kholina and the Estate of Igor Kholin
Translation copyright © 2017, 2018 by Ainsley Morse and Bela Shayevich
Illustrations copyright © 2017, 2018 by Ripley Whiteside

This translation is based on Arina Kholina's publication of Igor Kholin's diaries,
first published in *Zerkalo 41* (2013), and on poems published in *Izbrannoe* (NLO: Moscow, 1999).

The diaries appear with the permission of Irina Vrubel-Golubkina and Mikhail Grobman.
The poems appear with the permission of Liudmila Kholina and the Estate of Igor Kholin.

Eastern European Poets Series #40
Series Editors: Matvei Yankelevich & Rebekah Smith

ISBN 978-1-937027-99-5
First Edition, Second Printing, 2018

Ugly Duckling Presse
The Old American Can Factory
232 Third Street #E-303
Brooklyn, NY 11215
www.uglyducklingpresse.org

Distributed in the USA by SPD/Small Press Distribution
Distributed in the UK by Inpress Books

Design and typesetting by Don't Look Now! and Rebekah Smith
The type is Museo Sans Condensed and ITC Century

Offset printing and binding by McNaughton & Gunn
Covers printed letterpress at Ugly Duckling Presse

This book is made possible in part by a grant from the National Endowment
for the Arts and continued support from the New York State Council on the Arts.

Kholin 66: Diaries and Poems

Igor Kholin

translated from the Russian by
Ainsley Morse and Bela Shayevich

Igor Kholin

Kholin is lard.
Kholin is the wheel of a whetstone.
Kholin is the elbow of a shirt.
Kholin is the heart of a sheet of paper.
Kholin is the gut of a trough.
Kholin is the lip of a jackhammer.
Kholin is the god of the tram.
I understand Kholin.

* * *

Igor Kholin was born in Moscow in 1920, ran away from an orphanage in Ryazan, and eventually enrolled in a military academy in Novorossiysk. He barely survived World War II: a bullet that grazed the corner of his lips came out his back. He wore his scar as a permanent smirk, a wound that seemed to shape his voice. In 1946, authorities banned Kholin from Moscow after a fistfight in a soldiers' canteen and he ended up in Lianozovo, a suburb north of the city; it could have been a lot worse. In search of a volume by the half-forgotten and effectively forbidden Symbolist poet Alexander Blok, he made the acquaintance of a sympathetic librarian, Olga Potapova. She also happened to be an artist married to the poet and painter Evgeny Kropivnitsky.

Potapova and Kropivnitsky hosted a regular Sunday salon out of their meager, barracks-style apartment, fostering the work of avant-minded and pointedly un-Soviet emerging artists and poets, including Oskar Rabin, Genrikh Sapgir, and Vsevolod Nekrasov. Kholin quickly joined their ranks and began writing poetry in earnest. These poets and artists would come to form a loose poetry collective known (*post factum*, and controversially) as the Lianozovo Group. First and foremost, they considered themselves Kropivnitsky's students—and close friends.

Like his Lianozovo comrades, Kholin took the rough edges of Soviet life—the poverty, brutality, and rampant alcoholism—as primary subject matter, while lampooning formulaic Socialist Realist poetics. In a 1990 interview, he said: "For some reason that's always how it works out: no matter how fancy I try to be, no matter how formally inventive I get, I always still end up with realistic poems. [...] In my view, most of the Soviet poets who present themselves as realists are actually so abstract, rhetorical, and scholastic that they're really the ones that should be called formalists, not us."* Among the poets of his circle, he was known for his particular crudeness, simultaneously respected and condescended to for his lack of education. He had never made it past second grade.

The world in Kholin's poems, where abrupt death and abject penury inevitably cut down two-dimensional stock characters, was too coarse and inglorious to be considered poetry by official standards. Despite his efforts to defend and explain his work as "satirical" (Soviet aesthetic standards occasionally allowed satire as a form of "constructive criticism"), he could not publish in the Soviet Union until the late 1980s. So, like most of his fellow "unofficial" writers and artists, Kholin supported himself with odd jobs: children's book author, writing tutor, waiter, and, after the 1970s, antiques dealer.

The end of the Soviet Union did not bring about a boom in Kholin's literary career. He had enjoyed some fame

---

* Interview with Vladislav Kulakov, *Poeziia kak fakt* (Moscow, 1999), 321.

abroad from the mid-1980s, when he, Sapgir, and Nekrasov did a reading tour of Germany, Austria, and Switzerland. He also participated in readings organized in Moscow beginning in the early 1990s. However, Kholin's work—like that of many unofficial poets finally emerging into the light of official publishing—went largely unnoticed among all the material that began to be published after the dismantling of state censorship. Kholin was still an experimental poet, a creature ill-favored by the capitalist publishing industry and readership. He himself felt that the expanded possibilities for publishing were too little, too late: "I'm almost 70 and somehow I don't care anymore. It was also somehow supposed to happen earlier, when I wanted it, wanted to be published, to strut around as a poet with my chest sticking out…"*

Kholin died in Moscow in 1999.

* * *

Despite the sense of resignation the poet expressed in the early '90s, Kholin's literary star has risen in the years since his death. In 1999, his collected poems were published by the prestigious NLO (New Literary Observer), followed by his collected prose. His experimental novel *Koshki-Myshki* (*Catsie-Mousie*) was published for the first time in 2015, and a new collection of his diaries and prose is due to be published in Russia in 2017. Appreciation has grown for the biographical and poetic peculiarities that set him apart from many other heroes of unofficial literature (who tend to hail from

---

* Ibid., 323.

intelligentsia backgrounds and to have been raised from infancy on a rich diet of classic and forbidden literature). In his stubborn insistence on writing against all odds—poor education, limited range—Kholin seems to have occupied a unique stance with respect to the notion of the "Poet" in the Russian tradition. Personified by the nineteenth-century Russian poet *par excellence*, Alexander Pushkin, this largely Romantic figure has elements of the prophet, the philosopher, the activist, and the savior of *his* people. Kholin's early poems obscure the subject to a large degree; his later poems take a hyperbolically ironic view of the poet's role and significance, conditioned, of course, by his status as an unknown and unofficial writer. A bit later, the conceptualist poet Dmitri Prigov would adopt this style and turn it into a cottage industry. Due to these and other qualities, Kholin remains relevant—or productively problematic—for contemporary Russian poetry.

One aspect of Kholin's crassness that might distress today's readers is the occasionally unrestrained misogyny evident in his comments and observations on women.

> *Doesn't it seem to you*
> *Kholin*
> *That you're a creep*
> *No, I don't think so*
> *But maybe*
> *It's not such a leap*

Misogynist sentiments were not unique to Kholin, or even to his milieu. Indeed, Soviet society's vaunted sexual equality often meant that women held down full-time jobs while singlehandedly running their households—in

Russian this is known as "the double load." In any event, we decided to leave Kholin's (c)rudeness intact because it seems to constitute part and parcel of his self-positioning and character.

Regardless of his status and legacy, we the translators choose to take Kholin at his word: his poetry, and even more so his diaries, present us with a sense of his time and place—1966 in Moscow, Lianozovo, the barracks, filth and grim drudgery—all of which is far away from everything we know, yet as familiar as last night's un-emptied ashtray. Through him, we find ourselves waking up groggily back to back with an earnest, darkly funny, and tragically suppressed generation of avant-garde artists.

* * *

Excerpts from Kholin's 1966 diary were first published by his daughter Arina Kholina in 2013, in the Israel-based, Russian-language journal *Zerkalo*. The version presented here, though slightly abridged, is based on the *Zerkalo* publication with corrections and amendments from a manuscript of a forthcoming Russian publication of Kholin's diaries and other prose writings prepared by Ivan Akhmetev. The poems offered here come from Kholin's *Selected Poems* (NLO, 1999); we chose poems roughly contemporaneous with the diary. Our heartfelt thanks go to Irina Vrubel-Golubkina and Mikhail Grobman of *Zerkalo*, Ivan Akhmetev, and Liudmila Kholina.

We first read Kholin's 1966 diaries on the heels of translating Vsevolod Nekrasov (*I Live I See*, Ugly Duckling Presse, 2013), and concluded that the diary itself, as a portrait of Kholin's persona, might serve the Anglophone reader better than our attempts to match the rhythm of his almost exclusively rhymed poetry. Our friend Ripley Whiteside, most often a painter of landscape and wildlife, who had been doing a series of "Death Portraits" in homemade walnut ink, drew the pictures of Kholin's friends included here.

While the diary forms at best a partial portrait of Kholin, through these entries we seek to outline a window into the lost world of the post-Thaw Moscow literary underground. Our method was (truly) Method: we translated this book while staying in a mostly abandoned St. Petersburg apartment that was seemingly frozen in time: the refrigerator, "Peace" brand, was from 1937; there was a "Red October" piano; a century's worth of books stashed in every imaginable nook; and Stalin-era plumbing. After Bela's long days of sleeping or drawing, and Ainsley's long days of tracking down the remnants of 1960s and '70s-era unofficial literary life, we would convene in the kitchen, the hearth and heart of Soviet intelligentsia life. Here, Ainsley would sit in the easy chair while Bela lay on the floor. Ainsley would read a sentence from the diary and Bela would tell her how she thought it should be translated. This would get typed into the computer, and then we would argue. It was kind of like having a séance— living the Kholin lifestyle in a Kholin-esque environment, with Ainsley's morning sickness replacing the brutal hangovers. Kholin haunted the place and our process. We hope we've trapped Kholin's ghost.

— Ainsley Morse and Bela Shayevich

NOTEBOOK ONE

August 1966

6.*

Today was Yodkovsky's birthday. A mixed crowd. Ugly. Urin, Klabukov, Shlyonsky, etc.

Lots of booze. Yodkovsky got drunk before everyone else. It was all over by midnight. People read their dumb poems. I'm tired of this shit.

Earlier today I talked to Yodkovsky about moving out to his house in Iksha. He's charging a symbolic ten rubles, which is exactly how much he owes me.

7.

Sunday. Went to Iksha. Me, Kira Gur. and Fredynsky. It was hot as hell on the train. We were ready to drop dead. As soon as we got there it started pouring, we barely made it to the house. We ate and went to bed. Woke up. Went back to Moscow.

Edik [Yodkovsky]'s shack is a total wreck, but it's livable. Genrikh Sapgir came out. We met up in the evening. He wrote a great poem. A leap off a balcony.† Talked about art. With some poets form

Edmund (Edik) Yodkovsky (1932–1994) — a poet, writer and journalist. See his description of Kholin on page 46.

Viktor Urin (1924–2004) — a poet known for Futurist tendencies, began publishing in official periodicals in the 1970s.

Arkady Klabukov (1904–1984) — a children's writer and translator from Udmurt.

Vladimir Shlyonsky (1945–1986) — a poet and songwriter.

Iksha — suburb of Moscow; located about 30 miles north of the city.

Kira Gur[evich] Sapgir (b. 1940) — born Kira Gurevich into a family of literary lights; second wife of Genrikh Sapgir. She worked as a journalist, translator, and children's writer before emigrating to France in 1978.

Vladimir (Volodya) Fredynsky (b. 1937) — an artist with leanings toward folk art. Joined the Union of Artists in 1971.

Genrikh Sapgir (1928–1999) — Kholin's best friend. Prolific poet. Published widely in samizdat, Sapgir also had a career as an official Soviet children's poet.

---

* These numbers correspond to the dates of the month. Throughout the text, we've kept Kholin's idiosyncratic style for the dates of the entries.

† "A leap off a balcony" comes from the poem "Happiness" in Sapgir's late-1960s collection *Elegies*.

prevails over spirit. The opposite is better.

Poets don't experience reality as it appears, but rather as they feel it.

We went over to see Al. Dov. Gurevich. He's bright and cheerful. Enviable at that age. His wife looked drained, unclear why.

I'm moving to Iksha. I'd like to sell the table, the bed and the armchair. It'll make the move easier. Everything about country people is larger than life except for their brains.

8.

An incredibly even day. Didn't do anything. Went to the movies, *Some Like It Hot.*

America. Not bad. Called up Kira Gurevich. It turned out Genrikh was there, talked to him. Called up Kim Meshkov. I wanted to ask him to help move my stuff to Iksha. He's on vacation. Read Blok's diaries. Not so hot. Read *Science and Technology.* What a boring magazine. Didn't squeeze out a single thought all day, Monday.

9.

I took my furniture—the bed, the table and the armchair—to the consignment shop. They offered me next to nothing. I got the sense that the people who work at this store are hard-boiled shysters.

In the evening I called Oleg Tripolsky.

Al[exander] Dav[idovich] Gurevich (1906–1967) — Kira Sapgir's father, a translator and journalist.

Kim Meshkov (1935–1998) — official children's writer, screenwriter, and playwright.

Oleg Tripolsky (dates unknown) — artist; married to Rimma Zanevskaya, Sapgir's first wife.

Nikolai Karamzin (1766–1826) — important Sentimentalist writer and historian. The two-line poem is "Two Comparisons" (1797).

Then I read Karamzin:

> What is our life? A novel. The author is: Anon.
> We read it word by word, we laugh, we cry, doze off.

Brilliant lines. "Correction" is a beautiful poem too. Excellent poems: concise and eloquent.

The day went by smoothly. God willing!

10.

Today is not my birthday. However, I will be 47 soon. Old age? Oh yes! It's only when some eighteen-year-old girl looks at you that you become young again for a moment. You toss your head back like a young buck and walk past her. Lyrical? Lyrical!

Stupid? Stupid!

That's how I spent the sixth of August. Plus Fredynsky and I went to Gorky Park. We had two disgusting shish-kebabs at Kavkazsky, I saw my daughter, and later at Genrikh's we read Zakhoder's translations of Heine in issue six of *Novyi mir*. They were crap. Zakhoder is as talentless as a thousand devils.

The "No comment" section in the same journal. Firsov and Perventsev are horrible. Fyodorov's a moron. It was all bleak until we got to Omar Khayyam.

Half past one a.m. Tomorrow I leave for my voluntary exile in Iksha. Renting a room in Moscow is expensive. It's free in Iksha. Long live Yodkovsky.

Boris Zakhoder (1918–2000) — well-known children's writer, poet, and translator.

Novyi mir [New World] — one of the main Soviet literary journals.

Vladimir Firsov, Arkady Perventsev, Vasily Fyodorov — Soviet writers of Kholin's generation, loyal to the regime and Socialist Realism.

Omar Khayyam — eleventh-century Persian scholar and poet.

11.

Iksha. The village of Ignatyevo. Sapgir and Fredynsky are here too. Cognac. Canned ham. We went swimming in the canal. The air is clear and fresh. We drank. After Genrikh and Volodya left, I got to cleaning. I washed the floors and the dishes. The filth is otherworldly. Damp. I think it'll all be dry soon.

12.

Days in the village are monotonous. Got up around nine. Made myself millet for breakfast. I had it with margarine and sugar.

The village store doesn't have any potatoes, cabbage or milk—nothing.

I went to Iksha, that is, I walked over from Ignatyevo. I came back with 6 kilos of potatoes and a head of cabbage. I arranged to get my milk and eggs from some farmers in the village. Swam in the canal. Wrote a poem. Fickle summer.

The thunderstorm that night was exceptional. Non-stop thunder. I woke up and thought Moscow was getting bombed. Then I heard the rain.

I started working on getting my children's poems in order.

13.

Lived through another one. Village life is exactly like it was a million years ago. It's amazing how well savagery and civilization get along. For the most part people live in filth and poverty. There are tons of kids—they multiply like rabbits. Some of the people here are rich. Unbelievably stuck-up. My next-door neighbor is a drunken slob. He came by in the evening. Mumbling incoherently. I tried but couldn't understand a thing. Thank God! He's leaving soon. This morning I went to look for mushrooms in the woods. Didn't find many. I wrote a poem called "We Sowed Flour." The kids here don't play the same games as the kids in the city—here it's all about agriculture. I was walking by and heard one girl saying to another:

"Go to the pigsty!"

My other neighbor is a drunk too. He delivers groceries to the kiosk on horseback. He drank so much he couldn't tell his hand from his foot. The horse had to take him home.

14.

I didn't have time to write yesterday. Now it's the 15th.

Sapgir and Kira came up from the city. Out here I'm particularly happy when friends visit. They brought a bottle of cognac. Hot dogs, cucumbers and tomatoes. Kira immediately pounced on the food. An astonishingly ill-mannered woman. It's hard to look at her when she's eating. She stuffs hard-boiled eggs into her mouth whole. Puts her hands all over everything—and needless to say, they're filthy. Always dropping things. She can't do anything right. She cut the cabbage into such big chunks you couldn't even fit them in your mouth.

I wrote a children's poem, "My Neighbor." In the evening Genrikh and I read Rilke, a brilliant poet in an appalling translation. The two translations by Pasternak in the introduction are excellent. The rest was translated by some guy named Simkin, but maybe it was actually all Pasternak. Worthless. We also read this book by an economist, Tereshchenko, *American Experiments in Management.* Fantastic. All we have here are scum and scumbags. But what works for America won't work for Russia. That's as clear as day.

We went to bed at midnight. Kira left, Genrikh stayed.

Boris Pasternak (1890–1960) — Russian modernist poet. Banned from publishing after being awarded (and forced to turn down) the Nobel Prize in 1958, he continued to work as a translator, though like many translators often did not receive credit for his work.

Vasily Kliuchevsky (1841–1911) — historian of the pre-revolutionary period.

15.

Nice weather. Warm and sunny. Drowsy. Genrikh slept in, I got up at eight o'clock. We went to the woods. Picked a bunch of mushrooms. Fried them up for dinner.

We each wrote a poem. Mine was a children's poem, "Thank You, Car," Genrikh's was grown-up. A great poem. We read Kliuchevsky.

Contemplated the essence of existence. We live. Bacteria live in us. We eat living things (livestock). Bacteria eat us. We're alive below them and above them.

16.

Genrikh went back to Moscow. I walked him to the train station and saw him off. Then I went to the store and bought ten liters of kerosene, three kilos of carrots, and two tins of canned flounder. When I got home I conked out. Woke up after two p.m. Made lunch. Fried potatoes with lard and heated up yesterday's borsht. After lunch I wrote another children's poem, "Bigger and Smaller." In the evening I went to the mill that's in the church. The miller is my neighbor Egorovich. He gets 2 rubles[*] a ton. The cowherds get a kopeck per liter (approximately).

Read Dostoevsky til midnight—*Demons*.

17.

I remember that as a kid I was particularly sensitive to verbal insults.

I think that poems should adhere to three rules. They should be:

1) Formally solid.
2) Emotional.
3) Intellectual.

---

[*] A *ruble* was equivalent to about $6.25 in US dollars in 1966; a ruble contains 100 kopecks.

I came to these conclusions in part after reading a piece by Krishnamurti.

Both my neighbors were utterly drunk. One of them dragged the other one home on a horse. They're both around 70.

18.

I don't like property owners. But I have nothing against private property. How can I reconcile these two things within myself?

I'm writing children's poems every day. In the evening I walked over to Iksha. A raggedy little hamlet. At night I read Dostoevsky, *Demons*. A work of genius, despite the fact that he repeats himself in it.

19.

If I imagine something, that means that it exists for me.

Is there a line between reality and the imagination?

20.

Saturday. Nothing to write. Divine monotony. You fall into a certain rhythm. It turns out you don't need a thing. No women, no wine.

I'm writing children's poems.

Jiddu Krishnamurti (1895–1986) — popular Indian philsopher.

21.

1. Children's literature in its current state is unequivocally an applied art, insofar as

it has a prescribed moral. And unvarying form, and a fixed set of subjects.

2. Lack of personality. Any expression of individuality exasperates our lady-editors. More than anything else, they're afraid of futurist tendencies.

A person's psyche must not deviate from the norm. Humanity's had it up to here with mad geniuses. Enough.

22.

Children's poetry is built around performance. Children are forced to memorize poems. They're forced to recite them in front of grown-ups. This has to be taken into account. In children's poetry, rhyme has a completely different purpose than in grown-up poetry, you could even say the opposite purpose. It's bad if you can guess the rhyme in grown-up poetry. In children's poetry it's good. It makes kids happy when they can guess the rhyme. It becomes a kind of game.

I visited old man Kropivnitsky yesterday. He's sick. Heart stuff. I think it's nerves. 73—he's no spring chicken. Olga Ananevna feels fine. Cheerful.

We talked about Sapgir's poems. A lot. Kropivnitsky only acknowledges his early work, which is excessively literary, contrived, overly romantic, and all riddled with banalities like the face of a pockmarked crone. Although it definitely shows some talent.

Evgeny Kropivnitsky (1893–1979) — painter and poet; a teacher of Kholin, Sapgir, and other poets associated with Lianozovo. See Kholin's description on page 29.

Olga Ananevna Kropivnitskaya (1892–1971) — artist; married to Evgeny Kropivnitsky. Kholin met her when she was working as a librarian in a local library, and through her met Kropivnitsky, Sapgir, et al.

But in some sense Kropivnitsky's right. Sapgir's excessive lefty-ness gets in his way. It's important for everyone to figure out what works best.

Futurism is alien to Kropivnitsky. He doesn't like Khlebnikov, Pasternak or Tsvetaeva. He praised my long poem "The Globe." Not sure I believe him.

24.

In the morning I went to Moscow. Got sucked in right away. Driz was visiting Genrikh Sapgir. We went to "Baku." Ran into Prygunov and Vinogradov. Spent the evening at Anurova's. Natasha, Tsyferov's wife, had just had a baby, and this was our excuse for getting drunk. Anurova, Savchenko, and Eva Umanskaya were walking around practically naked.

Yulia Anurova is ugly, cruel, stupid and hates everybody. When everyone went home, I washed myself and went to bed with Eva, which I really shouldn't have done. Left me feeling disgusting. Around four in the morning Yulia showed up. I got my stuff and left, saying I'd come back the next day. I stayed in Genrikh's room in Alexander-Nevsky. Hell. Trucks and trams booming all night long right under the window. I only got two hours of sleep.

25.

The whole day was spent going around to various publishers. *Murzilka*,

---

Velimir Khlebnikov (1885–1922) — one of the founders of Russian Futurism.

Marina Tsvetaeva (1892–1941) — major modernist poet.

Ovsei Driz (1908–1971) — Yiddish-language poet and children's writer, translated by Sapgir.

Lev Prygunov (b. 1939) — actor.

Leonid Vinogradov (1936–2004) — Leningrad-based poet and children's playwright.

Yulia Anurova (dates unknown) — actress; wife of the film director Nikolai Rasheev.

Statsenko — unknown.

Eva Umanskaya (dates unknown) — poet and Kholin's occasional girlfriend.

Vozhatyi. Volodya Prikhodko is planning to leave the journal. Probably for *Litgazeta*.

At four I met up with my daughter. We walked around a little on Gorky Street.

Then I went back to Sapgir's. Spent the whole day there. Yu. Mamleev came by.

We argued about God. I voiced certain doubts as to the advantageousness of there being a single God. Since it negates the individual personality. Everyone should have their own God—therein lies the future.

I went back home to Iksha late.

26.

My stomach hurt all day. I kept sleeping.

27.

My stomach stopped hurting. In the morning I went to buy potatoes in Iksha. Met Tanya Libina on the bridge. She was on her way to my place. Where on earth did she get my address? From Sapgir, of course.

We fried some potatoes. Then we slept in separate rooms. She'd wanted to leave, but she ended up staying over. For some reason things didn't work out too well with her, even though we started off in the same bed. Genrikh didn't end up coming, even though he promised he would. Filthy and atrocious weather. Cold.

Murzilka and *Vozhatyi* [*Scout Leader*] — children's magazines.

Vladimir (Volodya) Prikhodko (1935–2001) — writer, journalist, and children's author.

Litgazeta [*The Literary Gazette*] — Soviet literary journal.

Yu[ri] Mamleev (1931–2015) — poet and prose writer.

Tanya Libina (dates unknown) — Mikhail Libin's sister; briefly Kholin's romantic interest.

September 1

It got warmer. Libina left. She sent over a girl named Valya. From Vilnius. Came all this way to find happiness in Moscow.

On August 30 I went to Moscow. At Genrikh's. I got held up and stayed the night. Plus I had to pick up my laundry. Now I remember why I got held up: it was Genrikh's sister Ellochka's birthday. Genrikh's relatives are a real freak show. Nothing at all like Genrikh. We drank, we ate. I went to bed with mademoiselle Valya. She played hard to get all night long. So boring. The next day, that is, the 31st, we took it easy. Watched *The Man Without A Passport* with Genrikh. Garbage. We even got a little upset. In the evening we got drunk. Besides Valya, there was Zhenya—Nol's girlfriend—and her friend Larisa, who sat there all haughty. The stone guest, as they say. They ate, they drank, they left. Later on Rita Kamyshova materialized. Her yapping was unyielding, even yappy Zhenya was cowed. Noise surged through my whole body. I left the room and fell asleep til morning.

I think all bad poems should be called Turkish, and all people should be called our relatives.

In the morning I bathed at A. Gurevich's place. When I was getting off the train in Iksha, I ran into Edik's mama, the actual owner of the house. I thought she'd kick

The Man Without A Passport [*Chelovek bez pasporta*] (1966) — Soviet spy movie.

Rita Kamyshova (dates unknown) — wife of Alexander Kamyshov, a painter and graphic artist.

me out. But everything worked out fine: she decided she trusted me completely. She left the keys. She'll be back in the spring. I can stay here till then.

Caught up on sleep. Now it's eight in the evening. A Hungarian orchestra is playing on the radio. Here's what I intend to do right now: take a walk. I'm going. See you tomorrow.

2.

What can you do, we often have to do things that are obviously wrong. Here's one that's equally unpleasant for everyone: combing your hair when it's tangled. But just try not doing it.

Sapgir has developed yet another stage of drunkenness. Reading poetry. We recall the three previous stages. One: kisses ladies' hands; two: I'm a genius; three: talks shit about everyone; and now there's poetry, too, a drifting stage.

The sun got frisky, its warmth is trickling off somewhere. Not toward our Earth. What I mean to say: autumn is here. You couldn't feel it til September 1st. Got to figure out the firewood situation. Edik's mama said I couldn't use her wood.

It's seven p.m. I'm going for a walk.

3.

An unshaven man and an uncleanly woman are one and the same.

June 6, 1966
The floors are as filthy as in a gov. office.

6.7.66
Speaking of the New Arbat. It's not a pity that it was built, but a pity it was destroyed.

6.7.66
There's nothing more elegant than flowers.

A few Russians who didn't want to be listening were listening to the poems. And one Frenchman, who wanted to listen, but didn't understand Russian.

"I'm younger than everyone," says one.
"Yes," says the other, "for a corpse you're still very young."

Among the people, talk usually circles around housing, drink, and food. Sometimes women.

6.25.66
In order to live forever you need to stop time.

7.9.66
Whenever I reach the conclusion that the essence of existence is impossible to fully comprehend, I start seeing red.

Saber-toothed guests.

New Arbat [Novy Arbat] — major avenue in Moscow; constructed between 1962–1968, necessitating the demolition of some characteristic narrow streets and small buildings of the Arbat district.

6.19.66

When a woman realizes that sex is pleasurable, she becomes a whore.

In art you have to lie with wild abandon.

6.10.66.

Women are mice in disguise.
Men are cats in disguise.

6.13.66

A poet who seeks perfection in others' work is worthless.

6.15.66

No matter what you say about a person, it'll all turn out to be true.

Every object, every planet, every person has its own orbit.

It's bad when people say true things about you. They can say as many untrue things as they like.

6.19.66

A stick has two ends. But one of them may be significantly thicker.

It's easier to pour out of a container than to pour into it.

Overpowering gall.
Gall bordering on the fantastical.

6.8.66

Kholin is lard.
Kholin is the wheel of a whetstone.
Kholin is the elbow of a shirt.
Kholin is the heart of a sheet of paper.
Kholin is the gut of a trough.
Kholin is the lip of a jackhammer.
Kholin is the god of the tram.
I understand Kholin.

———

You want my friend to teach you how to write poetry?

Beware—everything will come to you secondhand.

July 7, 1966

God is a philosophical concept.
God only has to do with morality.
We say, "Oh God, help us build this house!" By this we mean to imply not direct assistance, but moral strength.

6.7.66

What don't people talk about when they don't have anything to talk about.

———

Edgy-cheeky.

———

I'm inclined to believe that the primary moving force in our world is not egoism, but boredom.

6.6.66

Thoughts like scraps of old posters.

You can tell her profession just by looking at her.

Editors are the worst possible variety of human being. They know that we're dependent on them and they take advantage of it.

A Russian broad. She comes over. Spends the night and won't put out.
All you get out of a night with her is a workout.

Finished transferring old notes.

Sept 4

A poet should be a bit of a graphomaniac.
They said it would rain today—it's nice out now.

Sept 5

About Evgeny Leonidovich Kropivnitsky. My teacher. 73 years old. Met him in 1949. 17 years have gone by since then. He graduated from the Stroganov Art Institute in 1911. I think from the applied arts department. Or class, as it used to be called. He never went to war, neither the first nor the second one. Hernia. Knew a lot of hunger. During the revolution he and his father and mother left for Vologda. Because they were starving. But people there were starving too. They

Vologda — medieval city 280 miles north of Moscow, on the Vologda river.

Evgeny Kropivnitsky

went to Udmurtiya, and it was the same thing there. Met Potapova. Got married. Returned to Moscow. In Vologda he had lectured on music. For 10 years after art school he didn't paint, he wrote music. He started drawing after meeting Potapova. For those ten years after art school he wrote music.* In art school he'd studied sculpture. He worked as an art teacher. Accountant. Clerk. For many years he taught painting at the Zhdanov and Leningrad Pioneer Palaces in Moscow. Member of the Moscow Union of Artists. Then he was expelled in 1964 or 1965. He'll probably be reinstated soon. He knew Arseny Alving, Filaret Chernov, Yuri Verkhovsky—poets. And lots of artists. Children: daughter Valya, married to Oskar Rabin. And Lev, his son. The artist. Now he's retired. Everything I'm putting down here comes straight from Kropivnitsky himself. For the past 25–30 years he's lived in Dolgoprudny. Right by the ponds. Not far from the old estate. A little room. Cramped. No amenities. The outhouse is far away. The water's outside. Heated by a wood-burning stove. In 1936, probably under the influence of Filaret Chernov, he started actively working on his poetry, which he had written since childhood. But those poems were probably pretty feeble.

In 1936 he found his voice. A minor but

Arseny Alving (1885–1942) — poet and translator, a student of Innokenty Annensky, and an early mentor for Genrikh Sapgir.

Filaret Chernov (1878–1940) — defrocked monk, poet, and mentor for Evgeny Kropivnitsky.

Yuri Verkhovsky (1878–1956) – poet, translator, and representative of "classical Symbolism."

Oskar Rabin (b. 1928) — one of the figureheads of the Lianozovo school of painting.

Dolgoprudny (the name means "long pond") — village near Lianozovo.

---

* The repetitions in this section are Yodkovsky's own.

very colorful poet with a distinctive character. The life of the little man. Everyday miniatures. Very precise, very exact. Vivid.

> The pier. The ships
> Speed by like trotters
> The motorboats
> Cut through the waters
> The tent houses beauties
> And a sign for "Cream Cokes"
> There's vodka and beer
> And plenty of folks.

I don't want to say that this poem is perfectly characteristic of Kropivnitsky—no. It's just the first one that came to mind just now.

He has other kinds of poems too. Philosophical ones. But that's just worthless whining. Rehashing everything you can think of. It's surprising that such an intelligent and refined person doesn't see this.

The basic premise of this "philosophy"—"We're all going to die"—is stupid, though a fact. I tried to tell him this once. That resulted in him breaking off all contact with me. We didn't see each other for a year. Now I just keep my mouth shut when I don't like something. But still, he's a wonderful poet. Bold and new, even now, in 1966. But poetry is secondary for him. Painting comes first. Here, he's a peerless master. One of the very best artists. Among the ranks of Chagall, Tyshler, P. Kuznetsov, Larionov. He paints women's heads and women in general with particular tenderness. He's achieved extraordinary heights in this genre. No matter what he tries in painting, everything comes out great, even abstractions.

He thinks the most important thing in painting is color and picture. He's right a thousand times over. That's why there's no whining in his art. Just painting.

His painting is extremely schematic. No realism at all. No falsity.

He loves the Old Masters and doesn't like contemporary painting. He doesn't even acknowledge the talent of his own son-in-law Oskar Rabin. No, but he does pay him lip service, even praising him sometimes. But that's just him playing games. He loves the Peredvizhniki too. And the Impressionists. Surrealism and Expressionism are alien to him. And not only in painting, but in poetry too. No Khlebnikov, Pasternak, Tsvetaeva, none of them.

He lives modestly. Only the barest of creature comforts. Dresses modestly. For the most part he doesn't eat meat. Maybe because he doesn't have teeth.

He looks vigorous, despite frequent illness. Very mobile. Goes into Moscow a lot. Goes to all the official exhibitions. Even the bad ones. He recently went to see Shurpin's show, a terrible artist. Amazing

Kholin names an interesting range of early twentieth-century artists: modernist *Mark Chagall*, folklore-inspired *Alexander Tyshler*, impressionist *Pavel Kuznetsov*, and avant-garde primitivist *Mikhail Larionov*.

The *Peredvizhniki* (Itinerants) — group of realist painters in late nineteenth-century Russia that sought indepedence from the conservatism of academic painting. Their paintings often thematized social injustice and common people.

Fyodor Shurpin (1904–1972) — Socialist Realist painter.

spunk for his age. He came to visit me in Iksha recently. I wasn't home, so he went to see Sapgir in Moscow. That's how he is. 73 years old. Enviable. He's had many students. Yura Vasiliev and Oskar Rabin for art. Sapgir and me for poetry.

I owe everything to Kropivnitsky. When I first came to him I didn't know anything. Total lack of culture. He told me about poets and artists. Read me poems, took me to art shows.

He doesn't smoke or drink. Falls in love with girls all the time. His last love was Lilya Osmerkina, the daughter of the artist Osmerkin. Not much of a catch. She's a drunk. What did he see in her? I don't know. He suffered terribly. It seems like it's all over now. Thank God.

Short of stature. Has a limp (he got run over by a car during the war. He'd collapsed from hunger on the highway). Bright blue eyes. A bald head, speaks quietly and calmly. He says that he's irritable. But I've never seen it. For the most part, he's a kind person. I suspect, however, that he can be also be mean.

Blok, Sologub, Briusov, and Balmont are his favorite poets. From the 19th century, Pushkin and Tiutchev.

I've been staying in. Not writing much. Going to Moscow tomorrow. Might get some money. Yesterday I went to see Kropivnitsky in Dolgoprudny. Ended up

---

Yuri Vasiliev (1925–1990) — painter, sculptor, and book illustrator.

Alexander Osmerkin (1892–1953) — avant-garde artist associated with the "Jack of Diamonds" impressionist movement in the early twentieth century.

Kholin refers to the early twentieth-century Symbolist poets *Alexander Blok*, *Fyodor Sologub*, *Valery Briusov*, and *Konstantin Balmont*, as well as to two major nineteenth-century poets, *Alexander Pushkin*, and *Fyodor Tiutchev*.

staying til eleven. I've been sleeping an awful lot. I guess I need it. The weather's not bad. Lay out in the sun some today.

The little neighbor boy. 5 years old. The one I gave a poem to. About how naughty Piggy nearly burnt to death (it describes how Piggy found some paper and matches and almost set his house on fire). The boy also found some paper and matches and also tried to burn down his house.

Sept 11

Not a soul in the house besides me and the cat.

Yodkovsky Edmund Feliksovich. 33 years old. A towering hulk. A blueprint of a man. Overall a pretty decent person. However, his shortcomings exceed his positive qualities. My note about him will contain certain contradictions. Such is his nature.

Positive quality—he's kind. Negative —inhumane. Positive—he knows a lot. Negative—he's incapable of making sense of phenomena. To be more precise—he's not a thinking person. Messy. Eats for three. Clumsy. Bad dresser. Impossibly gross when it comes to women. I don't know how he gets away with it. But then again, that's the kind of woman he goes for. As they say: birds of a feather. I've never seen Yodkovsky with a smart woman. Except for his first wife Tamara Gromova. But she too had her limitations.

Though in the end it did dawn on her to leave him. Otherwise she'd have been miserable her whole life. His second wife, Marina, is as dumb as a doorknob. But she's still smarter then he is. He dumped her in the most inhumane way. It's the worst stain on his conscience. I'll tell how it happened. When he married her he couldn't take his eyes off her. Then things cooled off. She got pregnant. She was right about to give birth, and he left her. Just couldn't wait.

We asked him, "Why'd you leave her?"

He said: "I thought she was somebody, but she turned out to be a nobody."

You thought Marina was somebody? It's written all over her face: family and children come first!

The second reason was the baby. Would we be wrong in calling Yodkovsky a moron and a sleaze?

This Natalie of his is, to all appearances, a kind soul. But I feel sorry for her. Yodkovsky, the inveterate liar, is always conning her shamelessly. He promises a lot and never delivers. She's a pretty little female of the bourgeois species.

Here's the weird thing. He—Yodkovsky—has spent his whole life striving to be honest and considers himself as such. But you'd be hard pressed to find a more inveterate liar. He lies, of course, to justify his ungentlemanly behavior. That's about all he's good for. Lazy. But he has a lot of potential. If he could only come up with a big project and make it happen. As long as it has nothing do with literature. But he won't even try. He's just going to go on writing his poems. That's how these people are. They don't understand that not everyone is meant to be a poet.

I was over at his place the other day. While I was there he got packed and left for Adler. That's where his babydoll lives. I think he went to check and make sure she's not out whoring. There's another one of his traits. While he goes chasing after every skirt that swishes past.

His mother has disowned him. She told me herself.

Without a doubt, he's a despicable person. I don't care. It's his life.

Yodkovsky is direct. But his ingenuousness is covered in flies.

12.

It's raining lightly. Autumn. The trees are rusting and nothing has the strength to wash off all this rust. Farewell, summer, until we meet again, summer, until we meet again.

Yesterday, after a long hiatus, I went to see Oskar Rabin. He's cheerful and energetic as ever. He has a few new paintings. Valya does too. She hasn't been feeling well. Katya finished high school. Now there's the question of where she'll go next. The girl's a bad student. It's unlikely

Gennady Tsyferov (1930–1972) — screenwriter, playwright, and children's book author.

Platon Fidoseyev — unknown.

Valery Stigneyev (b. 1937) — photographer, curator, and teacher.

Vsevolod (Seva) Nekrasov (1934–2009) — concretist poet associated with Lianozovo.

SMOG (the acronym has varying interpretations, including "the youngest-ever society of geniuses") — short-lived and diffuse attempt to found an experimental, semi-official artistic movement in Moscow in the mid-1960s.

she'll get accepted at any university. It's very hard these days anyway.

I saw old man Kropivnitsky with Fredynsky and Tsyferov, accompanied by two young ladies. His wife came home from the hospital with their newborn son yesterday.

He said that I'm neurotic. This is a really popular word right now. If you get in a fight with your wife or your mother-in-law—you're neurotic. If you've just been bumming around—you're neurotic.

Yodkovsky is out of the loop. He hasn't heard of this word yet. I should tell him. Let him use it to his heart's content. Platon Fidoseyev and his wife were there too. She's ugly and has a limp. I envy people who can live with women like this. There was also a kid named Yura, his last name is Belyaev. Studies at the architecture institute. He paints. The kid's alright.

Saw Stigneyev. Gloomy as usual. He's even abandoned his wooden wit.

Saw Seva Nekrasov. Also gloomy. Two gloomy guys in one house. A bit much. They say the SMOG guys are going to have a convention. Officially. I doubt it.

I walked around for an hour and a half. The air was damp. But nice to breathe. Then it started drizzling again. I went home. I'm reading Kliuchevsky's *History*. About "Russian Truth."

Sept 13

Mayakovsky is a great Chinese poet.

September 14

What's more acceptable: a life filled with all kinds of stimulation, or a life of moderation.

For a thinking person, it's the life of moderation. Leaves a lot of time for reflection.

It's sunny, thank God. I ate. Going for a walk. Yesterday I wrote a poem, "Water" (for children). "Pigeons" the day before yesterday. Today I'm going to try to finish writing "Warbling."

Sept 17

People whose feelings are easily hurt always feel stupid. But not everybody is smart enough to admit it.

The paintings of Ilya Glazunov are like a woman past her prime: no good at all in the bright light of day. But in dim half-light she seems not half bad.

September 21

It's horrifying how fast time flies. It's cold. No rain today. A strong wind. Walked around a lot, slept a lot. I've been sleeping 12–14 hours a day. Maybe that's why time is galloping by so fast.

September 19 I was in Moscow. Saw Sapgir. An insatiable traveler, he had barely gotten back from the south and

Ilya Glazunov (b. 1936) — successful Soviet-Russian artist, whose paintings usually treat historical or religious themes.

was already taking off for Leningrad.

Turns out he had gone down south with a woman he knows from Riga named Lida. I know this Lida. I was actually the one who first made her acquaintance, but Sapgir has kept it up all this time. Love. Kira sniffed them out somehow and now she's a raving Fury. So Sapgir took her to Leningrad. To absolve his guilt. He's gotten very fat, which really doesn't look good on him. The way he puts on weight is weird—his face is spreading. He's still drinking a lot. But he still knows his limits. He was proclaiming some new ideas about poetry, but I don't remember anything.

There were four of us: Tsyferov, Kira, Sapgir and me. Plus Kira's parents—her mom and dad. Naturally, it was mayhem. They made it completely impossible to pay attention. But he was saying interesting things. About the Leningrad poets Brodsky, Gorbovsky, and Rein, the last of which no one likes, neither in Moscow nor in Leningrad.

Iosif (Joseph) Brodsky (1940–1996) — Nobel-prize winning poet; before he was expelled from the USSR in 1972, he belonged to a group of Leningrad poets known as "Akhmatova's orphans."

Gleb Gorbovsky (b. 1931) — Leningrad-based poet and children's writer.

Evgeny Rein (b. 1935) — poet from Brodsky's circle.

Kira Sapgir

NOTEBOOK TWO

9.24.66

It's cold. But the sun's out. Nothing to report. Went to get bread at the stall in Ignatyevo, there was no bread. The car broke down. Headed to Iksha on foot. Bought bread, apples and Bulgarian jam. So many people got on the ferry across the canal that it almost tipped over.

The Libins. Misha, his sister Tanya, Misha's wife Lena. They're all short. Misha and Tanya are fat. They both have wide faces. Lena has a little fox-face. All intellectually limited. Total absence of the capacity for thought. They're barely scraping by. Misha writes children's poetry, he's not bad, but writes very little. He works for either the Moscow or the regional department of culture, I don't know which one. Tanya studied violin at the conservatory in Leningrad and Moscow. Then she quit. Lazy. Got married to Shalonov.

9.25.66

It's eleven p.m. The day is over. There's a vile drizzle outside. I walked around for a couple of hours this afternoon. Wrote two poems for the traffic police administration. Read Rilke. It's warm in the house. We got the woodstove going. Going to Moscow tomorrow. Read Shershenevich. A strange poet. Original. But it's some kind of mix of vulgar cliché and real poetry.

Mikhail (Misha) Libin (1940–2004) — poet and children's writer.

Shalonov — unknown.

Vadim Shershenevich (1893–1942) — avant-garde poet with ties to primitivism and imagism.

9.27.66

Went to the traffic police administration yesterday. Handed in the manuscripts. Seemed like they liked them. At four I was at the House of Pioneers. One kid showed up. We talked. I told him about Russian poets starting with Simeon Polotsky. Got home after midnight. First frosts.

This morning there was a little rain. Strong winds. Slept til noon. Stoked up the fire. Got to find a room in Moscow. I got an earful from Nina Georgievna. Annushka Danziger called her up. Her ma grabbed the phone and started railing against me. Saying I'd corrupted her daughter. That's not true. I had only the best intentions. Taught her how to write poems. The rest she was born with. And thank God I kept my hands clean throughout. Annushka got married to a Nepalese man and is planning on leaving Russia. It's too bad, she could have been a good poet. Although to be honest, I've been getting disenchanted with her talent. They say she's pregnant now. Of course, that's the end of her poetry, most likely. She's not even 17 yet. Married and a kid.

October 4

Our thoughts about the future and the past are a time machine.

Evening. Yodkovsky came by. Picked up Marina's stuff. I couldn't help myself

---

The House of Pioneers — Soviet institution; a kind of cultural center for children and young people.

Simeon Polotsky (1629–1680) — Russian monk, dramatist, and poet whom some credit with laying the foundations for modern Russian literature.

Nina Georgievna — unknown.

Anna Danziger (dates unknown) — poet and ex-girlfriend of Kholin.

and started lecturing him again. Why do I keep doing this?

I spent a couple of days in Moscow. Nothing interesting at all. At the Children's Literature offices they gave me a review of my poems. The review is churlish. It couldn't have been written by anyone but Zakhoder.

The weather is mild. The height of autumn. *The Wick* paid me for my screenplay—150 rubles. Not much. They could afford to pay 300. They're taking bread right out of writers' mouths.

By the end of the month I'll have gotten 800 rubles. I have a hundred, I'll get three hundred more from the Litfond and join the co-op. I talked to my daughter about it. She thinks it's a good idea.

October 8. Saturday.

A little high society at Alisa Poret's. As usual, everything was very refined and consequently boring. The guests: me, Alyona Basilova, Magda the Pole—a literary scholar. She came to find out about the OBERIU poets. Tsyferov. I didn't know the rest of them. Alisa read her little stories. Very nice. Not much else to say about them. Got back to Iksha around three in the morning.

The Wick [*Fitil'*] — Soviet TV series featuring satirical short films.

Litfond [The Literary Fund] — founded in 1934 (along with Socialist Realism); sought to provide funds to needy writers.

Alisa Poret (1902–1984) — artist and children's book illustrator. In her youth, Poret was a friend of Daniil Kharms and other OBERIU poets.

Alyona Basilova (b. 1943) — poet associated with the SMOG group.

Magda the Pole — unknown.

The OBERIU poets — Informal collective who wrote experimental literature and children's books from the late 1920s–1930s, at which point they were all variously repressed. The group included Daniil Kharms, Alexander Vvedensky, and Nikolai Zabolotsky.

Oct. 17. Monday.

[The following entry is written in Yodkovsky's handwriting.]

Kholin, Igor Sergeyevich. 47 years old. Tall, gaunt, stomach problems. A cultured man, low-born. An autodidact (finished 2nd grade). The most brilliant incarnation of "black literature"—barracks poetry.

I have a positive opinion of him, although people say all sorts of things about him: that he served in the NKVD, beat a prisoner half to death and did time for it. If any of this is true, it's not his fault, it's the times. Positive qualities: a singular, severe worldview that manifests in both poetry and everyday life. For example: I went on for ages proving that Mayakovsky is "a great bad poet," while he summed it up in a single epigram: "Mayakovsky is a great Chinese poet." And he's like that with everything.

Negative qualities—intellectually limited. It's that provincial narrow-mindedness that results from insufficient education. He's a bit like Tarsis: for him, communists and fascists were one and the same, and for Kholin, many things in life are "tarred with the same brush"—he doesn't distinguish shades and nuances. Although, I repeat, in essence, he often turns out to be right because he sees the most drastic aspects of phenomena.

NKVD (1934–1946) — Soviet secret police at the height of Stalin's Terror; predecessor to the KGB.

Valery Tarsis (1906–1983) — Soviet Ukrainian writer; editor of the SMOG group's samizdat journal, *Sphinxes*. His writing exposed the practice of incarcerating dissidents in mental hospitals, and he was forced to leave the USSR in February 1966.

Positive quality—he's a moralist (in the lofty sense of the word); honorable in everyday situations.

Negative—he's bilious. For him "the whole world's a brothel and all the people are whores."

His personal needs are limited. Undemanding, practically ascetic.

He has bad luck with women. He and his wife split up a long time ago, the best he can do now is mademoiselles like Eva Umanskaya. He recently endured the greatest passion of his life—he fell in love with a model who, they say, dropped him for being penniless and impotent. A brighter spot was Anya Danziger, whom he treated like a daughter.

Hard-working. Is knowledgeable about painting and contemporary leftist artists.

I figure he'll remain an old bachelor.

The best thing he's ever made is a handwritten book, *The Work-Week on Earth*, about life in the barracks in Russia. He hasn't topped it yet—he's hampered by a general lack of culture. I suspect that he reads little and unsystematically, and gets most of his information from hanging out with better-read friends.

Kholin is a man with blinders on. The best lines he ever wrote are:

> ...the times are harsh:
> The poet is Kholin,
> The GenSec is Khrushchev.

In short, the poet doesn't fall far from the general secretary. And vice versa.

I think that his literary fate is to remain a second-rate children's poet because he'll never have the courage to publish his adult poems abroad—and anyway, no one would take them. Essentially, he's a representative of the homespun "school of bleakness." Rabin had the courage and the talent to make his name abroad, Kholin just doesn't.

If he could only meet a nice girl like Natalie, he'd be a lot happier. But he won't, and even if he did, she'd walk right past him. He's old.

It's not that I don't care about what happens to him, but how can you help a man who, at 47, still makes horrifying spelling errors? Who conceitedly overestimates his capabilities? Who doesn't understand the essence of editing?

Sometimes he's childishly trusting and open and happy to be alive. That's when I love him.

If war breaks out, I want my commanding officer to be Igor Kholin.

But his advice on writing is naive. Literature is not made by the semi-literate. Gorky also had a complex about being undereducated, but he managed to become the best-read man of his time. This is not going to happen for Kholin.

Is Kholin kind? I don't know. But perhaps he will forgive this intrusion into his diary.

Maksim Gorky (1868–1936) – writer and major figure of early Soviet literature; one of the founders of Socialist Realism.

[Note in the margins in Kholin's hand:
"These several pages are the best thing that Yodkovsky has ever written"—I. Kholin, 11.4.66]

November 4

What happened: Left Iksha. Moved into Lida Shevchuk's place at 1A Chistoprudny Boulevard, Apt. 55.* It snowed. The frost gaped. Three of my books came out. I'm filling out the paperwork for the co-op. Now I live near Tolya and Galya Brusilovsky. I started working at the Zhdanov district Palace of Pioneers. They pay me a solid 55 rubles a month. It was Gurevich's birthday, Sapgir and I read our poems to Nussberg and his friends. Recent exhibitions: Hokusai, Falk, Labas. Somebody started a rumor that I'm impotent. Tolya Brusilovsky went to Poland. Tsyferov got invited to go to Czechoslovakia. He didn't get the paperwork in on time. Gubanov seems to be back in the loony bin. A new decree about political hooliganism. Wrote nothing.

November 5

The room I'm living in is dark. I assembled a bed out of a mattress that I bought for 2 rubles, there's a 1 ruble table, 2 chairs for 50 kopecks each. Everything was so cheap because in Moscow there's

Anatoly (Tolya) Brusilovsky (b. 1932) — artist known for his work in collage, assemblage and body-art.

Lev Nussberg (b. 1937) — kinetic artist and experimental poet.

Alexander Labas (1900-1983) was an artist of the early Soviet avant-garde; his exhibition in 1966 was one of the first after a long hiatus following accusations of formalism in the 1930s.

Robert Falk (1886-1958) was a pre-revolutionary impressionist artist.

Leonid (Lyonya) Gubanov (1946–1983) — poet and *enfant terrible* associated with the SMOG group.

---

*   Kholin's new apartment is in a central location in downtown Moscow, near the Chistye Prudy metro station.

a store at Preobrazhenka that sells confiscated goods.

When Lyonya Gubanov came over he said that a person could go crazy in a room like this. Meanwhile, it's impossible to say what color the walls are. The paintings are revolting. The floor is filthy. The drapes haven't been cleaned in centuries. There's dust and filth everywhere. My landlady, Lida Shevchuk, is slovenly and fond of hitting the bottle. She has people over every day. She brings them all to see me. I end up having to leave the house. I don't have anything to say to them and I don't feel like trying. They're all ordinary folk. For the most part they moo rather than talk. Sheer horror. When can I get out of here?

November 6

I saw Brusilovsky. Just reeking of the sweet scent of Poland. Didn't skip a single pub. Lucky guy. Last night we were over at Kim Meshkov's. Me, Brusilovsky, Irena Yasnogorodskaya from Leningrad and some Novitsky with his wife, an overgrown knockout coquette. They work at the regional youth theater or something. Then this Yuri Aleksandrovich—he teaches at Patrice Lumumba University, he knows the language of the ancient Incas. Always trekking off to foreign countries. There was a lot of food. But it was all amazingly bad. The roasted chicken

Irena Yasnogorodskaya (b. 1942) — friend of Kholin and Sapgir; later involved in publishing the work of the "nonconformist" poets of the late Soviet period.

turned out to be half-raw. The coffee was gross. The pâté and the fish in aspic were store-bought. The only good thing was the vodka. Tolya was hitting on Irena. She's so short it's ridiculous. I slept with her a couple times a while back. Now I wouldn't go for it. I'm glad I restrained myself.

I forgot. S.M. Golitsyn and his wife were there too. A hopelessly bad writer. Kim's wife is getting on in years, but she looks fine. She's the lead director at that same youth theater. Everyone went home late. Around three a.m. Tolya and Irena left a little earlier, abandoning me to the whims of fate. I only read them my children's poems.

November 17

The holidays* were unremarkable. I didn't even get drunk. My landlady Lida and another girl and I went to this artist Volodya's place, near the Prospekt Vernadsky metro stop. We drank, we ate, we danced. Wait, actually I think we just drank. The other girl was skinny and not very tall. She has a lot of moles. The biggest one's on her back. Hairy legs. She's a little over thirty but her breasts haven't started sagging yet. I couldn't wait for her to leave in the morning.

Yura Bogorodsky brought her. He's an alcoholic and she dropped him for

---

* In the Soviet Union people celebrated the anniversary of the 1917 October Revolution in early November.

Sergei (S.M.) Golitsyn (1909–1989) — successful children's book author.

Yuri (Yura) Bogorodsky (dates unknown) — artist and illustrator of children's books, including Kholin's.

me pronto. She'd really had it with him. When he gets drunk, he becomes deeply uninteresting. As they say, a lump on a log. A real bummer. Yura just stands there all evening long blinking and repeating the same thing over and over again, "I'm somehow a bit sad today!"

And the girl needs intellectual stimulation, though of course, she's just a little bougie girl. What gives her away isn't the empty and stupid stuff she talks about—it's her hat, nobody wears bowler hats anymore. Not for a while now. But the bougie girls have only now started wearing them. Late to the party, which makes it easy to tell what she is right away. Nowadays you can tell a lot about a person by how they dress. A guy can wear a holey sweater and greasy jeans and be highbrow. You can tell he's sophisticated from a mile away. Meanwhile, brand-new clothes only emphasize the fact that you're a lowly bourgeois. Like for example right now metal jewelry has gone out of style, but a lot of people haven't caught on yet. In this day and age clothes are the only thing we have to judge people by. Our society girls are dumb, but you have to admit they know how to dress. Bogorodsky is the complete opposite. He's a slovenly dresser and he doesn't care. He's short and bald, which apparently causes him a lot of grief. He drinks, probably because he has low self-esteem.

As of now he's a mediocre artist, he illustrates children's books. Kitties and tigers.

The other day: Sapgir, Ball, Galya Demykina, Tolya Brusilovsky and I went to visit Gennady Aigi. He works at the Mayakovsky museum. But he lives at the back of beyond, out in Ochakovo. He used to live somewhere else. Had his own house or half a house. Then he got resettled. He's Chuvash—a good poet. I haven't read his poems. At his house, there was this book of Apollinaire's poems in French. At one point, I knew a couple of them in Annensky's translation. He also had a book of paintings by Filonov, the painter from Leningrad. It was published in Czechoslovakia. Aigi also played us a record of Aleksei Kruchenykh, the Futurist poet, reading his poems. The last of the Mohicans. A wonderful poet. It's too bad he's been completely forgotten, despite the fact that there was an event dedicated to him at this same Mayakovsky museum. He's forgotten anyway. His poems and fantastic essays have been out of print for a long time. I met him once. He's this little man. Worn down by life. Hard to believe he's still kicking. He read some of his poems. Reading them, the man completely transformed. He became young. All of a sudden, he was tall and animated. His voice is resonant, accustomed to performance. I also recently met the artist Boris Lavrov.

Georgii Ball (1927–2011) – writer and children's book author; married to Galina Demykina.

Galina (Galya) Demykina (1923–1990) – artist and children's book author.

Gennady Aigi (1934–2006) – experimental poet of Chuvash heritage; wrote in both Russian and Chuvash.

Innokenty Annensky (1855–1909) – late-Symbolist poet.

Pavel Filonov (1883–1941) – Leningrad-based artist of the late avant-garde.

Aleksei Kruchenykh (1886–1968) – central figure of pre-revolutionary Russian Futurism; founder of zaum language with Velimir Khlebnikov.

Boris Lavrov (b. 1938) – graphic artist; member of the Union of Artists.

Valya Vorobyov just stopped by.

On November 15 Genrikh Khudiakov showed us his poems over at Kira Gurevich's. They were great.

Sasha Laiko stopped by today. He read me some poems. They were better than the ones I'd heard before, a long time ago; many years ago he had a long hiatus, when he didn't write anything. Now he's started writing again. Praise the Lord!

November 23

In addition to all his other failings, Brusilovsky lacks basic tact. Yesterday I was on the phone with Driz. He said he couldn't invite us over to his house. Something was going on with his wife. I think she's sick. Brusilovsky immediately came up with his own interpretation.

"Some people are so greedy," he said, "not like you and me though, right?"

I didn't respond to that. He recently got a colossal studio. Two rooms, one larger, one smaller. Some lousy sculptor had it before Brusilovsky. He plastered all the walls with stucco to make it look like a grotto. It didn't work. Came out horribly tacky. I said as much to Tolya. Not sure he believed me. Whatever. He's the one who has to get by on his puny provincial intellect. At this point I have no choice but to make a small digression. As a rule, I tend to pay closer attention to the negative traits of my friends and people who

Valentin (Valya) Vorobyov (b. 1938) — painter, writer, and memoirist.

Genrikh Khudiakov (b. 1930) — experimental poet and visual artist.

Alexander (Sasha) Laiko (b. 1938) — poet and children's book author.

I come into contact with. For the most part, they're all good people. And, for the most part, they all have faults. In day-to-day life, I'm pretty tolerant. And it's only here in my notes that I let it all out. […]

Not long ago—November 20—we all got really drunk on the occasion of my friend Genrikh Sapgir's birthday. There was Genrikh Sapgir, Kira Gurevich, Oskar Rabin and his wife Valya Kropivnitskaya, Yulia Anurova (Rasheeva), her nine-year-old daughter Katya, Tolya Brusilovsky, his wife Galya, Alyosha Khvostenko (an artist from Leningrad), Eva Umanskaya—my former lover, and Tanya Bolshakova from the Modeling Office, who was posing all night like a top model. They're all so identical. It's horrible. They all have the same gestures, smiles. It's a good thing I didn't marry Valentina Filippova, now Sergeeva in her second marriage. Tanya Bolshakova is just as pretty. But because of those smiles and gestures I found her repulsive. Tsyferov and his wife Natasha were there too. Natasha is as sweet and pretty as ever. She's put on some weight since getting married, which really suits her. And she dropped those awful House of Fashion mannerisms. The menu: sandwiches with red caviar, ham, herbs, cheese and vegetable spread. There was also salad, grated turnip and red pepper. Roasted duck was the main attraction. The wine list included: pepper-infused

Aleksei (Alyosha) Khvostenko (1940–2004) — poet, singer-songwriter, and artist.

Tatyana (Tanya) Bolshakova (dates unknown) — Kholin's girlfriend.

Valentina Filippova / Sergeeva (dates unknown) — another one of Kholin's exes.

vodka, regular vodka and Gamza wine. It was an ordinary evening. Which is probably why I got drunk. I was the drunkest person there. Even drunker than Yulia Anurova. For the first time ever, Yulia didn't pull any stunts. Though she did get into a fight with her daughter. They riled each other up into some real hysterics. Yulia ran outside without a coat and lay down on a bench. I went out to talk her down. After that I became so drunk I don't remember anything else. I woke up in the morning in my room and turned on the light. Here is what appeared before me. A pool of vomit next to my bed. My suit and a lamp lying in it. My sheets were also covered in vomit. A cot against the far wall with Khvostenko sleeping in it. My head was coming apart like a badly-glued box. I felt like I was on a swing-set. I got up and cleaned up the vomit. But even afterwards there was a terrible stench in the room that lingered for a few more days. Khvostenko woke up too. I woke up my landlady Lida Shevchuk. We all threw in for a fifth of vodka and six bottles of beer. Khvostenko and I went to the store. Sapgir and Yan Satunovsky came over. We drank everything we bought. I started feeling better. Khvostenko told me that when we got home the night before, I didn't go to bed; instead, we went to see this unbelievably sophisticated lady named Aelita. She didn't let

Yan Satunovsky (1913–1982) — experimental poet and children's writer; later in life associated with Vsevolod Nekrasov and the Lianozovo group.

us in. I tried to get him to go somewhere else, but he refused and we went back to my place. Lida told me that I had a talk with her about our relationship. I told her that she's a good person, but that I wasn't going to sleep with her. Tolya Brusilovsky told me that I did a beautiful job setting up the cot for Khvostenko. I kept falling on it, getting up and then falling again. And getting up again, etc.

I have decided to sell the paintings I have.

I've been offered a place in a co-op in Vishnyaki, two rooms, 24 [square meters] total at 170 rubles/square meter. They've just started construction on the building. Should be completed in the first half of 1967. I have 1000 rubles. I need another 600. Where am I going to find it?

I called up G. Sapgir today. He's going to a Schoenberg concert. My daughter came by. She got 50 r. out of me for a collar. She's having a coat made. We went to the bank together. I came home. Lida made noodles—spaghetti. They've started selling it now. They say we bought a whole product line from the Italians. Really good noodles. I'm not liking the weather in Moscow right now: it's drizzling, dripping off the rooftops. 2–3 degrees Celsius. Khvostenko seems to have gone back to Leningrad. I didn't make an effort to get to know him. I have enough close friends to last me the rest of my life. I'm not

Genrikh Sapgir

reading Balzac anymore. I'm reading O. Henry. He has such tantalizingly precise plots. I like it. I wrote one grown-up poem today. Otherwise I'm not writing anything right now. And I'm even making an effort not to write.

November 26

Fredynsky, first name Volodya. A tall citizen with narrow shoulders. Black beard. Going for the priest look. In reality all of these external features are rooted in his wimpy little soul. That day—and this was two or three days ago—I was dragged over to his place by Gena Tsyferov. He was with a girl. She was unexceptional, a little Tatar. Tsyferov spent the whole night being neurotic. The little Tatar was hitting the bottle hard and felt like being kissed and hugged by everybody, not just Gena. The table was covered in comestibles. The satsivi gleamed with a nutty sheen, the lobio lay there modestly concealed, as if hiding from the guests. The quails, cut in two, basked on a great platter, surrounded by a ring-dance of the greens known as purslane. The vodka glittered in cut-glass carafes, towering above the table: as if to say, look at me, this is all good, but I am the empress here, and without me none of this—the satsivi and the lobio* and the red pepper

---

*   Satsivi (chicken in walnut sauce) and lobio (stewed kidney beans with cilantro) are classic dishes of Georgian cuisine, an important part of Soviet culinary culture.

and the quails—will go down your throat. And indeed: we took her at her word and began demolishing her mercilessly, slamming back shot after shot, despite the fact that in her immediate vicinity a bottle of Georgian champagne lay resting on ice. Everyone's tongue quickly loosened, but that did not make the conversation any more lively. Fredynsky was, as it were, the heart of the gathering: all eyes were on him. We drank to his health. Why? I don't know. It remained a mystery. When he was asked, he answered evasively: "Does it matter why we got together?" Maybe he's right, who knows. He pontificated all night long: "Ilya Glazunov (a fashionable artist) came by the other day, he said my paintings are good." Then an immediate digression: "Eat the satsivi first, then the lobio!" And again: "Ilya Glazunov said that when I have twenty paintings done, he'll get me a show at the Manezh." Basically, Ilya Glazunov came up about two hundred times. I remember that when Ilya Glazunov was still a total nobody, he used to drop Mikhalkov's name in exactly the same when whenever he could: "My mentor Sergey Vladimirovich said this-and-that." The guests at Fredynsky's: Tsyferov, his beloved, some Ernest with his wife Katya. Yura—Fredynsky's apprentice, also studies at the architecture institute—a worthless character, his last name didn't stay with me. And two more colorless characters. Man and wife. She kept wetting her lips with her tongue to make them more sensitive. Seems like it was working. She was stocky, like a workhorse. I wonder what it would be like if you put high heels on a horse?

Right now the Moscow intelligentsia is very taken with this game: you light a match and pass it around a circle. Whoever's holding the match when it goes out has to answer any question asked by the other players. We played this game. The fundamental limitations of these people are evident from the kind of questions they were asking: "How old are you?" "Who here don't you like?" "Who do you like best?" To break up the monotony, I asked one guy: do you masturbate? He answered that he did in his youth. And immediately became furious with me. I asked Fredynsky's beloved a question in an abstract language, something like aberdeh rukimeh eskeh tukimi cheloreh siliki? She didn't answer. Later I said that I was 33,000,145 years old, and they made me forfeit. In this game you're also supposed to forfeit if you can't answer the question. Everyone went home late. We went out and hailed cabs. No one was that drunk. We didn't even sing. Tsyferov and his lover (can't remember her name, and I'm too lazy to go look at the beginning of this entry) came over to my basement at Kirovskaya. I couldn't refuse him, and they spent the night at my place. I set up the cot for myself and went to bed. They sat down on the bed. Tsyferov started making the moves on her. I pretended to be asleep. She was resisting, fighting him off, but silently. I watched them through a slit in the blanket. He hitched up her skirt, and things got a little more interesting. Then they turned out the lights and I fell asleep. I woke up a couple of times, and they were still at it. They finally left around six in the morning. She never did give in. Now I remember, her name is Roza, she works in animation. I told Tsyferov that he should ask me ahead of time before he comes over again.

Why do I keep a journal? Probably for practice. I don't break the entries up into paragraphs in order to save space. As soon as I started writing this entry, I mean the one for today, six or seven Leningraders showed up. Irena, back again from Leningrad with her husband Rudek, Lyalya with her conductor husband. Some guy named Markin, a composer, and another one. Lyalya's husband (who everybody calls Yashka) came for a conductors' competition. I'll finish writing tomorrow. I'm tired. The time is probably around two in the morning on November 28th.

Rudek Yasnogorodsky (dates unknown) — Irena Yasnogorodskaya's husband.

December 8

And so time moves forward, sometimes lazy, sometimes frolicking. December, cold. No snow to speak of. I joined the cooperative, that is, I made my first payment, 40% or 1670 rubles. This is a huge amount of money for me. My hands were shaking when I made the transfer at the bank. But what else could I do, I don't have anywhere to live. They're kicking me out of Lida's basement. The other day a precinct police officer came by with an inspector from the housing office (which is now called ZHEK). They were royal jerks. I told them so but I shouldn't have. They gave me two weeks to move out. The artist Valya Vorobyov has started coming to see me regularly. He's supposed to get a studio on Shchepkin street soon. That street used to be called Third Bourgeois St.* He promises to let me stay there as soon as he gets it. My daughter came by the other day, all abloom. I'm still working at the Palace of Pioneers (if you can believe it). The girls—Shilova and others—have started going to Edik Shteinberg's place on Wednesdays. Some Vitya—a prose writer—goes with them. No one knows what he writes. Valya Vorobyov and I made up a game: a list of patented brides. We married off Volodya Serebriany, who arrived from Vilnius.

Irina (Ira) Shilova (1937–2011) — film scholar.

Eduard (Edik) Shteinberg (1937–2012) — painter and philosopher.

Vladimir (Volodya) Serebriany (dates unknown) — artist from Vilnius, Lithuania.

---

* Kholin may be referring to Abram Room's 1926 film, *Bed & Sofa* (Russian title: *Third Bourgeois St.*).

We've been taking him around to people's houses. We were over at Irina Edelman's the other day. Drinking. We're supposed to do something tomorrow too. I got a call from Diafilm. They want me to sign a contract. I have to write a screenplay for 40 frames. They'll pay 100 rubles. Yuri Mamleev came by. He had a lot of interesting stuff to say. Tolya Brusilovsky came by. We went by his studio. Now it's one o'clock in the morning.

Irina Edelman (dates unknown) — artist.

Diafilm — form of instructional multimedia (silent filmstrips with separate recorded soundtracks) popular in the Soviet Union. Kholin refers to the eponymous studio that produced most of these materials.

POEMS

* * *

She died in the barracks at age 47—
No kids.
She was a men's bathroom attendant.
Why did she live?

* * *

They met at the Taganka stop.
He spent the night at her apartment.
He's a funeral bureau accountant
She's a nurse in the birthing department.

* * *

Someone tossed out burlap sacks,
Someone splattered out their dregs,
Ugly portrait on the fence,
And below in chalk: "Oleg"

Two guys squabbling by the barn,
One's already started roaring.
A holiday. In early May.
In the barracks life is boring.

* * *

Bunch of garbage by the fence
And the neighbors take offense:
"Wouldn't you know it, Egor's hussy
Went and left the yard all messy."
From the fence the women flew,
Egor's wife was black and blue.

***

A windowsill, some sweet décor,
The flowers getting watered;
Downstairs around the corner store
The boys are getting blotto;
Meanwhile the neighbors down two doors
Are beating up their daughter.

* * *

Not allowed on the subway—visibly plowed
Outside, the fog was a thickening cloud
He slumped on the sidewalk, as if in a trance
While he was passed out, they made off with his pants

* * *

You may think
This shining
Object
Is a washing
Machine
I'm not what I seem
I'm a poet
The only
Man on Venus
My parents
Are loudspeakers
My buddies
Are light switches
My best friend
Is a blender

* * *

Martian girls are hotties
Charming
Obliging
Bodies
Custom made of
Nuts
Bolts
Nickel-plated
Legs
Just the best
Enameled
Breasts
Two
Irregularities:
1. Their heads are shaped like
Bottles
2.Their genitalia are
On the backs of their heads

***

A martian couple
She's
A milk jug
He's
A hub cap
Not a bad chap
A poet
No privates
Instead
A smooth spot
They manage copulation
Through wild gesticulation

***

Dear Genrikh Veniaminovich[*]
You failed to show
Again
As we'd agreed
So the whole night
Was pissed
Away with wasted Ovsei Driz
And equally off
Tsyferov
I have nothing
Against women
Or wine
But Tsyferov
And Ovsei
At the same time
Is overwhelming
But that's not the thing
The thing
Is that I'll see you anyway
If not tomorrow, then yesterday

---

[*] The poem mentions three of Kholin's friends referred to in the diary, the poets and children's writers Genrikh Sapgir (his patronymic is Veniaminovich), Ovsei Driz, and Gennadi Tsyferov.

* * *

Men of art
You need broads
To intensify your sensations
Yes
Or else you're cold
As toads
Yes
Men of art
You need freedom
To release your sensations
Yes
Or else you stray
Like dolts
Yes
There's no rush
Our era is harsh
The poet is Kholin
The GenSec is Khrusch

* * *

One guy says
I'm a genius
I say
Sure
That's definitely true
Others say
I'm a hack
And I agree with that
A third says
I killed a guy
Indeed, I nod
Everything people say about you
Is the truth
Woven
From nothing

* * *

You don't know Kholin
And I don't recommend him
He's such a bitch
And such a whore
His head's
An empty bucket
His poems
Make you vomit
Instead of legs
There's crutches
Stuck up his butt
Got no skills, pays no bills
Yet he eats for five
How does the good earth
Keep this beast alive

***

Doesn't it seem to you
Kholin
That you're a creep
No, I don't think so
But maybe
It's not such a leap

* * *

Look at that
Kholin's face
Is melting
As if hail
Were pelting it
His ear is sliding
Down his side
His cheekbone slides
Along his thigh
His thigh is flowing
Into a pail
There's a hole in the pail
I'm sloshing
He cries
All over my
Galoshes

* * *

You hear the beat
Of retreat
Kholin
Is leaving
Kholin
Is ending
Anyway
Who's to say
It could be anything
Maybe Kholin
Isn't destructing
Maybe Kholin
Is resurrecting

* * *

Kholin has horns
On his back
You want to
See them
Stand back
I'm removing my britches
Hands
Off
Bitches

* * *

If you're looking
At Kholin
And you see Kholin
Beware
They're pulling your leg
If you're looking
At Kholin
And you see 34 to the power of 35
Kholin is here

* * *

This bottle of wine
Is for Kholin
That's why
It was made
This pile of
Shit
Is for Kholin
That's why
It was laid

* * *

Kholin envies everyone
The ones
Who whistle
The ones
Who bristle
The ones
Who make it work
The ones
Who're brainless jerks
The ones
Who smile
The ones
Who go the extra mile

* * *

I'm putting my last name
On display
I'm ready
To say it
One million times
Kholin Kholin Kholin Kholin
Kholin
Kholin
Kholin
Kholin
Kholin's immortal
Kholin's immediate
Kholin
Number one poet
In the universe

* * *

I am stupefied
By the number of
Kholin's wives
Dina
The dummy
Vera
The vampire
Skinny
Sonya
And Lazy
Lena
Then Nina
With that mother-in-law
And Jiggly
Jenya
Plus Katerina
Who had
His son
And Alla
Who'd come
All the way from Riga
Galya
And Raya
The one from Uruguay
And the Malay
A wife
From every clime
This
For a man past his prime

* * *

Can you smell
That? Kholin
Reeks something awful
Something
Who knows what
People
Are wrinkling
Their noses
How can you bear
This stink
What do we do
Overboard
With him
Into the drink

* * *

Say
What's Kholin's deal
He
Squeals
Like a hog
Sprays spit
Thinks he's the
Shit
Can't get along with anyone

* * *

Where in the world is
Kholin
Kholin
Is ill
His life's a squiggly line
While yours
Is just fine
Yes
No debate
We live straight

* * *

Kholin broke his leg
Thank God
Nothing
Against him, but
May he break
His neck
May he break
His back
May he
Son of a bitch
May he
In the next life
And in this one
May his children
May he be
Buried alive
May he
Fall down the toilet
May he
Choke to death on shit

* * *

I'm alive
But it feels
Like
I'm in
Saliva

Igor Kholin was born in Moscow in 1920. He ran away from an orphanage in Ryazan, enrolled in a military academy in Novorossiysk, and was twice wounded in World War II. In 1946, he was dismissed from the military and exiled from Moscow for slapping a drunken comrade-in-arms. Kholin landed in a labor camp in Lianozovo, a suburb of Moscow, where one of his friends was the guard and would occasionally let him out to visit the Lianozovo library—he'd started writing poetry. When he asked to check out a book by forbidden poet Alexander Blok, he aroused the interest of the librarian, Olga Potapova, an artist. Potapova and her husband, the poet and painter Evgeny Kropivnitsky, invited Kholin to their Sunday salon for the young artists and poets (including Genrikh Sapgir and Vsevolod Nekrasov) who became known as the Lianozovo Group. Unable to publish his poetry in the Soviet press, Kholin barely supported himself with writing for children's magazines and odd jobs: writing tutor, waiter, and, after the 1970s, antiques dealer. His writing became more widely known during *glastnost* and after the fall of the Soviet Union. Kholin died in Moscow in 1999.

The Eastern European Poets Series from Ugly Duckling Presse (Selected Titles)

0. *The Gray Notebook* | Alexander Vvedensky
1. *Attention and Man* | Ilya Bernstein
2. *Calendar* | Genya Turovskaya
3. *Poker* | Tomaž Šalamun
4. *Fifty Drops of Blood* | Dmitri Prigov
5. *Catalogue of Comedic Novelties* | Lev Rubinstein
6. *The Blue Notebook* | Daniil Kharms
7. *Sun on a Knee* | Tone Škrjanec
8. *Less Than a Meter* | Mikhail Aizenberg
9. *Chinese Sun* | Arkadii Dragomoshchenko
10. *Iterature* | Eugene Ostashevsky
11. *The Song of Igor's Campaign* | Bill Johnston, tr.
12. *Do Not Awaken Them With Hammers* | Lidija Dimkovska
14. *Paper Children* | Mariana Marin
15. *The Drug of Art* | Ivan Blatný
16. *Red Shifting* | Alexander Skidan
17. *As It Turned Out* | Dmitri Golynko
18. *The Russian Version* | Elena Fanailova
19. *Dreaming Escape* | Valentina Saraçini
23. *The Life and Opinions of DJ Spinoza* | Eugene Ostashevsky
24. *What Do You Want?* | Marina Temkina
25. *Parrot on a Motorcycle* | Vítězslav Nezval
26. *Look Back, Look Ahead* | Srečko Kosovel
27. *Try a Little Time Travel* | Natalie Lyalin
28. *Thirty-Five New Pages* | Lev Rubinstein
29. *On the Tracks of Wild Game* | Tomaž Šalamun
30. *It's No Good* | Kirill Medvedev
31. *I Live I See* | Vsevolod Nekrasov
32. *A Science Not for The Earth* | Yevgeny Baratynsky
33. *Compleat Catalogue of Comedic Novelties* | Lev Rubinstein
34. *Blood Makes Me Faint But I Go for It* | Natalie Lyalin
35. *Morse, My Deaf Friend* | Miloš Djurdjević
36. *What We Saw from This Mountain* | Vladimir Aristov
37. *Hit Parade: The Orbita Group* | Kevin Platt, ed.
38. *Written in the Dark: Five Poets in the Siege of Leningrad* | Polina Barskova, ed.
39. *Elementary Poetry* | Andrei Monastyrski FORTHCOMING
40. *Kholin 66: Diaries and Poems* | Igor Kholin
41. *Letter to the Amazon* | Marina Tsvetaeva
42. *Moss & Silver* | Jure Detela